D0734897

Sisters
Make Life
More
Beautiful

ISBN: 978-1-68088-184-4

█ and Blue Mountain Press are registered in U.S. Patent and Trademark Office. Certain trademarks are used under license.

Printed in China.
First Printing: 2017

⊕ This book is printed on recycled paper.

This book is printed on paper that has been specially produced to be acid free (neutral pH) and contains no groundwood or unbleached pulp. It conforms with the requirements of the American National Standards Institute, Inc., so as to ensure that this book will last and be enjoyed by future generations.

Blue Mountain Arts, Inc.
P.O. Box 4549, Boulder, Colorado 80306

Sisters
Make Life
More
Beautiful

Written and Illustrated by
Heather Stillufsen

Blue Mountain Press™
Boulder, Colorado

Side by side
or miles apart,
sisters will *always*
be connected by
the *heart*

Sisters make
the *good* times *better*
and the hard
times *easier*

True *friendship* is in
the *heart* and *hand*
of a sister

Sisters *share*
sweet
moments

Words to describe a *sister*...

strong

hardworking

kind

lovable

talented

capable

beautiful

smart

brave

unique

A little *sister* time
is good for the *soul*

Sometimes,
having *coffee*
with your sister
is all the *therapy* you
need

Sisters *have*
the
most fun

Sisters *believe*
in you
even when
you don't

Sisters
always carry
love and *kindness*
with them
wherever they go

A sister
is someone
who *always* stands
beside you

Sisters
don't let
anything or
anyone
stop you from
going after
your dreams
and reaching *your*
goals

Having a sister
warms the soul…
and fills your heart
with *happiness*

A sister
is a *shoulder*
to lean on

Sisters make
the *best* memories

Sisters keep in touch
and are *always*
there for each other

Sisters make *life*
more *beautiful*

Sisters
are
forever
friends

About the Author

Heather Stillufsen fell in love with drawing as a child and has been holding a pencil ever since. She is best known for her delicate and whimsical illustration style, which has become instantly recognizable. From friendship to family to fashion, Heather's art

Photo by Christine E. Allen

demonstrates a contemporary sensibility for people of all ages. Her words are written from the heart and offer those who read them the hope of a brighter day and inspiration to live life to the fullest.

In addition to her line of greeting cards, Heather's refreshing and elegant illustrations can be found on calendars, journals, cards, art prints, hand-painted needlepoint canvases, and more.

She currently lives in New Jersey with her husband, two daughters, and a chocolate Lab.